To: Doneen
with love
From
Rachel
x

GW00706172

Silver Linings

A Ray of Hope & Promise

Written and Compiled
by Sarah M. Hupp

INSPIRE

Inspire Books is an imprint of Peter Pauper Press, Inc.
Spire is a registered trademark of Peter Pauper Press, Inc.

For photo credits and permissions
please see pages 80-81.

Designed by Taryn Sefecka

Copyright © 2004
Peter Pauper Press, Inc.
202 Mamaroneck Avenue
White Plains, NY 10601
All rights reserved
ISBN 0-88088-431-2
Printed in China
7 6 5 4

Visit us at www.peterpauper.com

Silver Linings

A Ray of Hope & Promise

Introduction

Was I deceiv'd or did a sable cloud
Turn forth her silver lining on the night?

JOHN MILTON, *Comus*

Dark clouds on the horizon usually signal a storm on the way. Struggles and problems also bring stormy weather to our own lives. Even when the tempest is at its height, however, silver linings around the clouds may shine forth, illuminated by the sun behind. So too, when we face times of trouble and doubt, our faith in God will help us find the way. We can again reach the blue skies of hope and faith and the sunshine of happiness, deep in the silver linings of God's loving care.

S. M. H.

Weeping may
endure for a night,
but joy cometh
in the morning.

PSALM 30:5 KJV

He who sends the clouds can easily clear the skies. Let us be encouraged—things are better down the road.

CHARLES SPURGEON

The most beautiful examples of hope often spring from our most difficult days, in the harshest of times. Hope blooms in the humblest of places.

When we face life's problems, God's silver lining of hope assures us that all will be well. Troubles may come, but when they go, we may find unexpected wonders that God has left behind. Knowing this, we can walk by faith and live in hope even through the stormiest of times.

Whatever comes,
let's be content withall:
Among God's blessings
there is no one small.

ROBERT HERRICK

Our present troubles are quite small and won't last very long. . . . So we don't look at the troubles we can see right now; rather, we look forward to what we have not yet seen. For the troubles we see will soon be over, but the joys to come will last forever.

2 CORINTHIANS 4:17-18 NLT

Even from a dark night songs
of beauty can be born.

Maryanne Radmacher-Hershey

In a thousand trials, it is not just five hundred of them that work "for the good" of the believer, but nine hundred and ninety-nine, *plus one*.

GEORGE MUELLER

As flood waters swirled around his Iowa home, Steve Sandusky realized that the farm that had been in his family for generations would be lost to the raging water.

On the seventh night of rain, Steve huddled with friends, listening to his CB radio. A call came over the radio that a nearby housing complex was threatened by the flood. Many in the area responded, but Steve was the first to arrive in his boat, braving the high winds and chill water. He rushed to the aid of Sheri Lovett, a local school teacher and piloted her to safety.

After Sheri had dried off, she shyly offered to take Steve out to lunch to thank him. As things sometimes go in small towns, it wasn't long before the two were dating regularly, and then became engaged. Less than a year after the flood, on a beautiful May day, the two were married.

"I thought I lost everything in that flood," said Sandusky, "but really, I have gained so much more. Sheri is the best thing that ever happened to me. Really, I've been blessed."

JOHN BEILENSON

Fill up the hours with what will last;
Buy up the moments as they go.
The life above, when this is past,
Is the ripe fruit of life below.

HORATIUS BONAR

[We can live] about forty days without food, three days without water, about eight minutes without air . . . but only one second without hope.

HAL LINDSEY

Hope remains the highest reality, the age-old power; hope is at the root of all the great ideas and causes that have bettered the lot of humankind across the centuries.

RONALD REAGAN

May the God of hope
fill you with all joy and peace
as you trust in him, so that
you may overflow with hope
by the power of the Holy Spirit.

ROMANS 15:13 NIV

Trials are only to test your faith,
to show that it is strong and pure.
It is being tested as fire tests
and purifies gold—and your
faith is far more precious to
God than mere gold.

1 PETER 1:7 NLT

When God is going to
do a wonderful thing,
He begins with a difficulty.
When He is going to do a
very wonderful thing, He
begins with an impossibility!

CHARLES INWOOD

When things
get rough, remember:
It's the rubbing that
brings out the shine.

E.C. McKENZIE

He prayed for riches that he might be happy;
He was given poverty that he might be wise.
He prayed for power that he might
have the praise of men;
He was given infirmity that he might
feel the need of God.
He prayed for all things that he might
enjoy life;
He was given life that he might
enjoy all things.
He had received nothing that he asked for—
all that he hoped for;
His prayer was answered—he was
most blessed.

AUTHOR UNKNOWN

Never give up,
for that is just the
place and time that
the tide will turn.

HARRIET BEECHER STOWE

Never despair in bad times; enjoy the good times when they come. For one true fact is clear: nothing stays the same forever.

God's children do not
know what the future holds,
but they know the One who
holds the future, and in whose
hands reposes all power in
heaven and on earth.

AUTHOR UNKNOWN

The hopeful man sees
success where others
see failure, sunshine
where others see
shadows and storm.

O. S. MARDEN

All which
happens through
the whole world
happens
through hope.

MARTIN LUTHER

Wait till the darkness is over,
Wait till the tempest is done,
Hope for the sunshine, hope
for the morrow,
After the storm has gone.

God is always working for our benefit, always bringing His grace and mercy into every situation. Though rough weather may come our way, nothing will deter God from His ultimate plan for our well-being. Our faith will carry us through the most difficult times, to the blue skies we know are only just ahead. As we trust and follow Him, God will reveal the silver lining of His grace and the fulfillment of His promise.

Do not fear, for I am with you;
Do not anxiously look about
you, for I am your God. I will
strengthen you, surely I will help
you, Surely I will uphold you with
My righteous right hand.

ISAIAH 41:10 NASB

God knows how to lead
us to the point of crisis,
and he knows how to
lead us through it.

AUTHOR UNKNOWN

God finds

a way
for what

none foresaw.

EURIPIDES

Each of us may be sure
that if God sends us over
rocky paths, He will provide
us with sturdy shoes. He will
never send us on any journey
without equipping us well.

ALEXANDER MACLAREN

How good it is that when our
faith wavers, God does not change
His mind or purpose for us.
He moves right on in infinite
love toward the final good.

G. CAMPBELL MORGAN

God knows the way that I take;
when he has tested me,
I will come forth as gold.

JOB 23:10 NIV

We stand in life at midnight;
we are always on the threshold
of a new dawn.

MARTIN LUTHER KING, JR.

All my hope on God is founded;
He doth still my trust renew,
Me through change and
chance he guideth,
Only good and only true.

ROBERT BRIDGES

How often we look upon
God as our last and feeblest
resource! We go to him because
we have nowhere else to go.
And then we learn that the
storms of life have driven us,
not upon the rocks, but into
the desired haven.

GEORGE MACDONALD

God moves in a mysterious way
His wonders to perform;
He plants his footsteps in the sea
And rides upon the storm.

WILLIAM COWPER

How much lighter trials become when we realize God's grace is twofold. It is not only the happy ending. It is also the peace we can feel during a painful journey, when we trust in God—all the way.

Doris Haase

M y widowed mom was a single parent who barely had time to sit down to eat a meal, much less plan "family time." Although my siblings and I were all expert laundry-folders and sandwich-makers, we all longed for more time with Mom. Our wish was granted in a strange and wonderful way.

Mom suffered a broken leg one day at work. She'd need to be off her feet for six weeks! Mom had no choice but to hire a housekeeper to help out. Suddenly Mom was putting together jigsaw puzzles and watching old movies with us. Her bedroom became our haven when we arrived home from school. The laundry piled up, but that didn't seem so important any more.

Someone said to Mom, "I bet you can't wait to go back to work!" Mom smiled and answered, "Yes and no. It may sound funny, but I'm glad I have a broken leg." "That broken leg was a blessing in disguise. It gave me the opportunity to see—to really see—the fine people my children are becoming."

After that, even after returning to work, Mom always seemed to have more time for "family time."

VIRGINIA REYNOLDS

God has marvelous ways of taking our worst tragedies and turning them into His most glorious triumphs.

JOSEPH STOWELL

God tempers the wind
to the shorn lamb.

LAURENCE STERNE

Art thou weary, tender heart?
Be glad of pain!
In sorrow sweetest things
will grow,
As flowers in rain.
God watches; thou wilt
have the sun,
When clouds their perfect
work have done.

ADELAIDE PROCTER

We know that all things work together for good to them that love God, to them who are the called according to his purpose.

ROMANS 8:28 KJV

When you go through deep waters and great trouble, I will be with you. When you go through rivers of difficulty, you will not drown! When you walk through the fire of oppression, you will not be burned up; the flames will not consume you. For I am the LORD, your God.

ISAIAH 43:2-3 NLT

I once saw a dark shadow resting on the bare side of a hill. Seeking its cause, I saw a little cloud, bright as the light, floating in the clear blue above. Thus it is with our sorrow. It may be dark and cheerless here on earth, yet look above and you shall see . . . a shadow of His brightness whose name is Love.

DEAN ALFORD

If we had no winter, the spring would not be so pleasant; if we did not sometimes taste of adversity, prosperity would not be so welcome.

ANNE BRADSTREET

Active faith gives
thanks for a promise,
even though it is not yet
performed; knowing
that God's contracts
are as good as cash.

MATTHEW HENRY

When Sir Harry Lauder's only son was killed in World War I, he said to a friend: "When a man comes to a thing like this, there are just three ways out of it— there is drink; there is despair; and there is God. By His grace, the last is for me!"

Do not so look upon your troubles as to forget your mercies.

THOMAS WATSON

All God's dealings are
full of blessing: He is good, and
doeth good, good only, and
continually. . . . Hence we may be
sure that the days of adversity,
as well as days of prosperity,
are full of blessing.

J. HUDSON TAYLOR

Until the storms and difficulties
allowed by God's providence
beat upon a believer again
and again, his character appears
flawed and blurred. Yet the trials
actually clear away the clouds
and shadows, perfect the form
of his character, and bestow
brightness and blessing to his life.

HUGH MACMILLAN

Take Joseph. What could have seemed more apparently on the face of it to be the result of sin, and utterly contrary to the will of God, than the action of his brethren in selling him into slavery? And yet Joseph, in speaking of it said, . . . "God meant it unto good." . . .

It was undoubtedly sin in Joseph's brethren, but by the time it had reached Joseph it had become God's will for him, and was, in truth, though he did not see it then, the greatest blessing of his whole life.

HANNAH WHITALL SMITH

"I know the thoughts that
I think toward you," says
the LORD, "thoughts of
peace and not of evil, to give
you a future and a hope."

JEREMIAH 29:11 NKJV

Keep your face
to the sunshine
and you cannot see
the shadow.

HELEN KELLER

Joy is the characteristic
by which God uses us to
re-make the distressing into
the desired, the discarded into
the creative. Joy is prayer—
Joy is strength—Joy is love.

MOTHER TERESA

The difficulties of life are intended
to make us better—not bitter.

E.C. McKenzie

I avoid looking
forward or backward,
and try to keep
looking upward.

CHARLOTTE BRONTË

A jewel is a bit of ordinary earth which has passed through some extraordinary experiences.

AUTHOR UNKNOWN

Whenever you find yourself disposed to uneasiness or murmuring at anything that is the effect of God's providence, look upon yourself as denying either the wisdom or goodness of God.

WILLIAM LAW

Seek to cultivate a
buoyant, joyous sense
of the crowded
kindnesses of God
in your daily life.

ALEXANDER MACLAREN

65

God is our refuge and strength,
A very present help in trouble.
Therefore we will not fear,
though the earth should change
And though the mountains
slip into the heart of the sea;
Though its waters roar and foam,
Though the mountains quake
at its swelling pride.

PSALM 46:1–3 NASB

Two people looked out from afar.
One saw mud; the other a star. . . .

In the pursuit of the fullness of
human life, everything depends on
this frame of reference, this habitual
outlook, this basic vision that I have
of myself, others, life, the world, and
God. What we see is what we get.

JOHN POWELL

The joy and peace of believers arise chiefly from their hopes. What is laid out upon them is but little, compared with what is laid up for them; therefore the more hope they have the more joy and peace they have.

MATTHEW HENRY

There is no danger of developing eyestrain from looking on the bright side of things.

AUTHOR UNKNOWN

You can't have rosy
thoughts about the
future when your mind
is full of the blues
about the past.

E. C. McKenzie

When times are good, be happy; but when times are bad, consider: God has made the one as well as the other.

ECCLESIASTES 7:14 NIV

Merrill Womach had been a gospel singer for many years prior to a fiery airplane crash in 1961 that left his face charred beyond recognition. The work of plastic surgeons repaired enough of the damage so that Womach could speak and sing again. Yet the scarring on his face was disfiguring. Friends thought that his public life was over.

Instead, Womach's popularity grew. "God has given me a face that people never forget," he insists. "Once they have heard what I have to say to the glory of the Lord, they never forget the face of the man who said it." Womach's face may be deeply scarred, but his outlook reflects the beauty of one who trusts God to make all things good.

The real legacy of my life
was my biggest failure—that I
was an ex-convict. My greatest
humiliation—being sent to
prison—was the beginning
of God's greatest use of my life;
He chose the one experience
in which I could not glory
for His glory.

CHARLES COLSON

A positive outlook that captures the soul is powerful enough to transform the bleakest of circumstances into the richest of blessings.

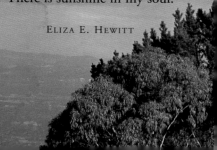

There is sunshine in my soul today,
More glorious and bright
Than glows in any earthly sky,
For Jesus is my light.
O there's sunshine, blessed sunshine
When the peaceful, happy moments roll;
When Jesus shows His smiling face,
There is sunshine in my soul.

ELIZA E. HEWITT

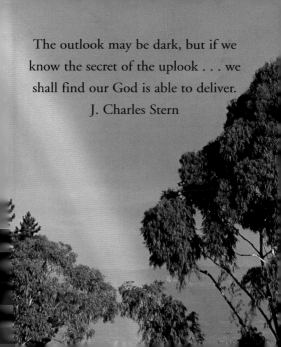

The outlook may be dark, but if we
know the secret of the uplook . . . we
shall find our God is able to deliver.

J. Charles Stern

There are no
difficulties with God.
Difficulties wholly
exist in our own
unbelieving minds.

THOMAS CHARLES

I sing because I'm happy,
I sing because I'm free,
For His eye is on the sparrow,
And I know He watches me.

CIVILLA D. MARTIN

Photo Credits